WHAT IT MEANS TO BE...

PROUD

Written by
Nancy Prasad

Illustrated by
Steve Pileggi

A proud person likes herself or himself.

One Monday morning, Ms. Barclay asked her grade one class to write about what they were proudest of.

Dylan was wearing his "Incredible Me" T-shirt that his grandfather had brought back from Florida. It gave him a great idea.

After lunch the students read aloud what they had written. Some of them talked about their pets or hobbies. Others discussed how good they were at singing or art. Then it was Dylan's turn. He grinned as he got up to read his poem.

I'm Proud to be Me.

I'm special.
I'm original.
I'm remarkable.
I'm incredible.
There's nobody else in the whole wide world
Just like me!

Everyone clapped. Dylan sat down smiling.

It is important to be proud of yourself—just because you're you.

A proud person knows that appearances aren't everything.

Janice was having lunch at Hannah's house one Saturday. "My grandparents are coming to visit," said Hannah. "I've got a new dress to wear."

"Do you want me to help you get ready?" asked Janice.

"Okay."

The two girls put their dishes in the dishwasher and ran up to Hannah's room. She put on her purple dress and Janice tied the bows in her hair. Hannah twirled around her bedroom and curtsied.

"Beautiful, simply beautiful!" cried Janice.

Hannah found her patent shoes in the back of her cupboard.

"They look a little dusty," noted Janice.

"There are some old cloths in the bathroom," said Hannah.

Janice wiped off Hannah's shoes. Now Hannah was ready to see her grandparents.

The girls went out to the backyard where Hannah's cat was chasing butterflies. Suddenly he ran right up a tree after one.

"Smokey, come down," called Hannah.

Smokey looked at her and meowed loudly. He seemed too scared to climb down the tree.

"What should we do?" asked Janice.

"He'll come down if I'm here," explained Hannah. She stood at the bottom of the tree and felt her shoes sinking into the soft dirt. "Come on."

Smokey meowed again and climbed down. Hannah held him and stroked his fur. "Good cat," she said. She put him on the grass.

Just then a car pulled into the driveway. Hannah looked down at the smudges on her dress and the mud on her shoes. "Oh no!" she wailed.

"Don't worry," said Janice. "They'll understand that you were helping Smokey."

"But I look terrible!"

"Hannah, your grandparents came to see *you* not your pretty clothes," explained Janice.

Hannah grinned. "I guess you're right."

It's natural to want to look your best. But remember that it's not how you look, but what you are that's important.

Be proud of younger brothers and sisters.

"Guess what?" Tammy said one night as she and Colette were getting ready for bed. "We're doing the play *Cinderella* at Kids' Klub and the tryouts are next week. Oh, I really want to be Cinderella!"

"I can help you practice for it," suggested Colette.

With Colette's help, Tammy started thinking, feeling and acting like Cinderella. One day she even streaked her face with dirt and didn't brush her hair.

"What a mess!" said her mother. "You better wash your face and brush your hair before supper."

"But I can't, Mom," explained Tammy. "I'm Cinderella."

Her mother laughed. "Well, Cinderella, how about sweeping the floor and washing the dinner dishes?"

Tammy was about to say no. Then she thought, "If that's what Cinderella had to do—that's what I should do too." So she said, "Okay, Mom."

The night for the tryouts arrived. "Good luck!" called Colette as Tammy left the house. "Hope you get the part!"

After Kids' Klub, Tammy came home later than usual. She had been walking very slowly and feeling sad. Colette had been watching for her out the living room window. She ran out to meet Tammy. "Tell me all about it."

Tammy's face crumpled. "I didn't get the part of Cinderella," she cried. "I have to be a mouse."

"That sounds like fun," said Colette. "You love animals. You'll make a cute mouse."

"You must think I'm awful not to get the part of Cinderella," sobbed Tammy, "especially when you helped me so much."

"I think you're great whatever part you play," said Colette, putting her arm around her sister. "You'll always be Cinderella to me."

Younger brothers and sisters often feel that they will never do things as well as you do. You can help them feel good about themselves by letting them know that you are proud of them no matter whether they win or lose.

Proud people do the best job they possibly can.

Ryan's father had been away for a week and the
grass in the front yard had grown very high.

"Let's surprise Dad and cut the grass before he
comes home," suggested Ryan's older brother
Cameron. "I'll cut and you can rake the grass into
piles."

"Okay," said Ryan.

Around and around Cameron pushed the lawn
mower, cutting in smaller and smaller circles. Ryan
followed him, raking the cut grass into neat piles.
He had been raking for about fifteen minutes when
Bobby came riding by on his bike.

"Come and play with me when you're finished,"
called Bobby.

Ryan raked faster and faster. He forgot about
doing a good job and trying to please his father. He
just wanted to finish so he could play with Bobby.
In a few minutes, he threw down his rake. "I'm
going now," he called to Cameron. "I've done my
part."

"We still have to put the grass into bags," Cameron reminded him. "You're not going to leave the job half done, are you?"

Ryan groaned.

"Come on, it won't take long if we both do it together," said Cameron. "We started out well. Let's finish the job well too."

When their father walked in the door that night, he was smiling. "Someone did a great job on the front lawn."

"Not some *one*—some *two*," said Cameron. Ryan laughed.

"I couldn't have done it better myself," said their father.

The way in which you work tells people a lot about you. If you take pride in your work, you will always try to do your very best.

**Proud people are pleased with their friends'
accomplishments as well as their own.**

"Live many lives! Enter other worlds! Read
books!" Ms. Barclay wrote on the blackboard.
Then she explained that it was reading month and
that there was a prize for the student who read the
most books.

"Coming to the library?" Kim asked Colette
after school. "I'm going to stock up on some
books."

"Not today," replied Colette. "I'm busy.
Anyway, we have four weeks to do the reading."

Kim went to the library alone and came out with
her arms full of books.

"So many books!" exclaimed Eva when she saw
Kim. "You're going to read them all?"

Kim nodded her head. "There are so many kinds
to try. There are animal stories, riddle books, fairy
tales—and that's only the beginning."

"Hmmm, maybe I'll go to the library with you
next time," said Eva thoughtfully.

Kim read books to her little brother Lee. She read instead of watching TV. And she read some more before she went to bed.

"Don't you think you're working too hard for this reading competition?" asked her father.

"It's not work," said Kim. "It's fun!" And she added another title to the list of books she had read. She even wrote "great," "good," or "not bad" beside each title. "That's to help the other kids when they want to choose a book," she explained to her father.

When it was time to hand in their book lists, Kim's list of twenty-five books was the longest. She won a gift certificate for a nearby bookstore.

"I can start my own library!" exclaimed Kim.

"Congratulations, Kim," said Colette. "You're my best-read friend! Um, could you help me find a good fairy tale to read tonight?"

"Sure, I know some great ones," replied Kim, looking at her list.

You are probably good at some things, while your friends are good at other things. Friends are proud of each other's successes.

A person can be too proud.

Colette's mother took Eva and Colette to the local ice skating rink one afternoon. The girls put on their skates and held hands as they went around the rink.

"Oooh!" cried Eva. "This is fun."

"I love skating to music," added Colette.

They skated for a while, then stopped to watch an older girl doing tricks in the middle of the rink. She skated backwards, then did leaps and spins. When she was finished, the people around her started to clap, but the older girl didn't even smile. She held her head high and skated away.

"I wish I could do just one trick," said Eva longingly.

"Look, she's coming this way. Let's ask her if she'll show us one," suggested Colette.

"You skate so beautifully," Eva said shyly to the older girl. "Will you show us how to do an easy trick?"

The girl gave them a scornful look. "I've got better things to do than teach you how to skate," she sneered. "I've won lots of awards!"

Eva and Colette were too amazed by the girl's rudeness to speak.

"Now scram!" she said. "You're in my way." And she skated off, holding her head even higher in the air.

"She certainly isn't as nice as she skates," Eva commented.

Just then the girl lost her balance and fell in the middle of a spin. A few people snickered.

"I'd feel bad for her," remarked Colette, "if she hadn't been so snooty."

No one likes to be with you if you boast or look down on others who aren't as talented as you or if you are unwilling to help when asked. A willingness to help others learn what you know shows that you aren't too proud.

Older people are often proud to be asked to talk about their lives.

Mitchell was walking by Mr. Martin's house one Sunday when he noticed a huge pile of odds and ends on the lawn. "He must be cleaning out his garage," Mitchell thought.

He came closer and saw Mr. Martin dusting off a heavy harness. "What's that?" asked Mitchell.

"This is Daisy's harness," answered Mr. Martin. "I found it tucked away in the garage. I'm going to clean and polish it till it looks like new."

"Daisy must have meant a lot to you," said Mitchell. "Who was she?"

"Daisy was the horse that pulled the milk wagon in the old days when I delivered milk," explained Mr. Martin. "I can show you some photos if you're interested."

"Sure," replied Mitchell. "I think my class would be interested too. Every week we invite someone to our classroom to talk. Would you come and talk about delivering milk with Daisy?"

Mr. Martin beamed. "I'd love to."

A few days later, Mr. Martin wore his old milkman's uniform to Mitchell's kindergarten class. He carried the polished harness and some photos. He told the children how milk and cream used to come in glass bottles and how he delivered it to people's doors every day in a milk wagon pulled by his horse.

"Daisy soon memorized my route," Mr. Martin said. "She knew which houses to stop at and what streets to take. I hardly had to guide her. She was smarter than some people I know."

Mr. Martin help up the blinkers Daisy used to wear on the side of her eyes so she wouldn't be distracted by cars and trucks. Then he showed some of his photos: Daisy wearing her feedbag full of oats, children feeding Daisy apples and sugar cubes, and Daisy and Mr. Martin together.

After the talk, everyone crowded around him to ask questions about Daisy. "I think you love Daisy almost as much as I did," said Mr. Martin, smiling.

Older people are proud of the things they have done. If you give them a chance to talk about their life, you will find they have many interesting stories to tell.

Proud people do not do things that would make them feel ashamed.

Joey liked to hang around a group of older boys who called themselves the Heroes. One day on the way home from school, he was trailing along behind the gang when they met some little kids carrying their drawings.

"Kindergarten baby, wash your face in gravy," chanted the older boys.

The younger children looked frightened and started walking faster.

"Let's have some fun," suggested the leader of the gang, as he walked up to the nearest child. "What's that you've got?" he asked, pulling the drawing out of Mitchell's hand. Then he let it fall. "Oops, I dropped it," he laughed. Then he stomped all over it.

The other boys started throwing the children's drawings in the air and laughing as they scrambled to get them.

"Join in the fun," said one boy to Joey. "You want to be part of our gang, don't you?"

Joey noticed that most of the kindergarten kids were crying by now. "You're being mean," he said to the gang members. "You're bigger than them and you know they can't fight back."

"We're just having some fun," muttered an older boy.

"It's not fun to make little kids cry," said Joey firmly.

"Whose side are you on anyway?" asked the leader. "I thought you wanted to be one of the Heroes."

"You're not heroes. You're bullies," stated Joey. He started to help the small children pick up their drawings.

"Are you one of them?" asked Hannah tearfully.

"No way! They're not my friends anymore," said Joey. "Come on, I'll walk you home."

It's hard to feel proud of yourself when you are taking part in something that is mean or petty. You feel proud when you are helping others, not when you're hurting them.

Being proud means honoring your heritage and helping to keep it alive.

It was Heritage Day. Booths selling food and crafts from around the world were set up in the town square. Banners were flying, bands were playing and people were wearing the clothes depicting their cultural heritage. Eva had on an embroidered German dress, Kim had a silk kimono, and Colette was in a Scottish kilt. They were deciding what to eat.

"Let's have some Korean food ," suggested Kim.

"And apple strudel for dessert," added Eva.

"Don't forget the ravioli!" Bobby reminded them.

They watched some folk dancing while they were eating. Then they heard some music from across the street. It was loud and fast and made them want to dance.

"It's reggae!" exclaimed Bobby. "Let's go see who's playing."

When they got closer, they gasped. It was Dylan and his father with their friends. Dylan smiled and waved at them. "I'll meet you later," he called.

"What a wonderful day," sighed Colette as they walked home. "The food was delicious, and the music was fantastic. It sure would be dull if everyone looked and talked the same way and ate the same food."

"That's what I like about this country," said Eva. "I can enjoy all kinds of new things here and I can also enjoy the customs of my homeland."

"I like seeing how other people live," agreed Kim.

"In that case, come over to my house and I'll show you the photos of my trip to Italy," suggested Bobby. "My grandmother took a picture of me in front of the Leaning Tower of Pisa."

"Does it really lean?" asked Eva.

"Come and see," said Bobby.

If your family came to Canada from another country, you are probably proud of your heritage. It is good to have an opportunity to share the customs that make it special for you.

People are proud of their pets.

"Next week is Pet Week," Miss Foster told her kindergarten class. "How shall we celebrate it?"

"I want to see everyone's pets—not just talk about them," suggested Janice. "Let's bring our pets to school!"

"Yes," agreed Hannah. "We could see one pet each day."

"That's okay for the little animals," said Mitchell. "But dogs need lots of room. Let's have a dog show Friday afternoon in the gym."

Everyone was happy with that idea. Then Miss Foster suggested that they invite the grade one class to bring their dogs too and ask people from the community to act as judges.

Everyone wrote the name of their pet on a piece of paper and put it in a hat. At the end of the day, Miss Foster drew the names of the pets that would be coming to school next week.

"Guess what, Fergie?" Tammy whispered to her hamster. "You're going to school on Monday." Fergie squealed and ran around on his wheel.

On Monday morning, Tammy's mother drove her and her hamster to school. "I'm so excited, Fergie!" exclaimed Tammy as she walked into her classroom.

Miss Foster put a name tag on Fergie's cage, and when it was time, Tammy told the class what he liked to eat and the games he liked to play.

The next day, it was Hannah's turn to show her cat Smokey. She had spent hours brushing him and he looked fluffy and beautiful. "This is his favorite toy," said Hannah. "It's a catnip mouse." When she threw it, Smokey chased after it. Then he rolled onto his back and played with it in his paws.

The following day Mitchell brought his pet salamander Humphrey to show everyone. He told them what Humphrey liked to eat. Then he let people touch the salamander's cool damp skin.

At last it was Friday afternoon. The kindergarten and grade one classes gathered in the gym.

Janice looked at the other dogs, then patted Nipper. "You may not be a special breed," she whispered, "but you're special to me." Other people seemed to think so too and came to admire Nipper.

Ryan and Joey stood together with their dogs: Red and Muffin. "I'm glad our dogs are friends," said Joey.

At the end of the day, Miss Foster said, "Does anyone want to trade his or her pet for anyone else's?"

"No way!" they all shouted.

If you take good care of your pet, you have a right to feel proud when others show an interest in it. It is good to have a healthy pride in yourself, your friends and the things you do. Here are some ways you can show this pride:

- Let younger brothers and sisters know that you are proud of them.
- Give others praise for doing something well.
- Never do anything that makes you feel ashamed.
- Always try to do the best job you can.